SPIDERS

Photo-Fact Collection

Scientific Consultant
Jennifer Gresham
Director of Education
Zoo New England

Copyright © 2012 Kidsbooks, LLC
3535 West Peterson Avenue
Chicago, IL 60659

Printed in China
011201001SZ

Visit us at **www.kidsbooks.com®**

Crab spider

CONTENTS

Amazing Arachnids

Down in the basement or up in the attic, out in the desert or high in the mountains—spiders are everywhere. And they have been here on Earth for more than 380 million years. There are about 30,000 known species, and maybe as many as three times more yet to be discovered. Spiders can be as big as 10 inches across or smaller than the head of a pin.

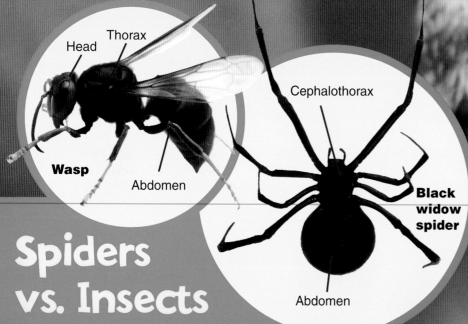

Head

Thorax

Wasp

Abdomen

Cephalothorax

Black widow spider

Abdomen

Spiders vs. Insects

Spiders are arachnids. They have eight legs and two main body parts—a cephalothorax and an abdomen. Insects have six legs and three body parts—a head, thorax, and abdomen.

Jumping spider

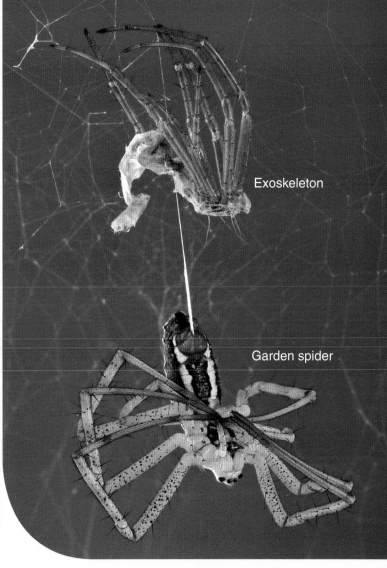

Exoskeleton

Garden spider

Break Out

Spiders have an exoskeleton on the outside, a tough suit of armor called a carapace, which protects the soft body parts. When a spider grows, its exoskeleton does not—it molts instead.

Deadly Dentures

A spider's mouth is double trouble for prey. On each of its two jaws, a sharp curved fang carries a poisonous bite. Then, on each side of the mouth are leglike things called pedipalps, or palps, which are used to hold prey.

Fangs

Pedipalps

Sensitive Body

Spiders have truly unique bodies. They are able to sense their surroundings and detect potential prey and predators with their ultra-sensitive appendages. For example, since spiders lack ears, they do not hear as humans do. But they have legs that do a lot of "ear-work." Mostly on the legs, but also on the body, are hundreds of tiny slits that sense vibrations.

Cross spider

Liquid Diet

Liquids are all that spiders can eat, so they have to turn their prey to juice. With their fangs, spiders inject victims with venom, then with digestive fluids. The prey's soft insides become like soup, and spiders can then suck up their meal.

Crab spider

Hanging On

A spider's legs are tools for balancing. Each one is flexible, with seven sections connected by joints. Web builders have three claws on each leg, while wandering spiders only have two claws.

Golden silk orb spider

Eye Sight

Most spiders have eight eyes, though a few have six or four or fewer. Web builders have poor vision. But some hunting spiders can see well in several directions at once, like the amazing wolf spider.

9

Garden spider

Lifeline

Whenever they travel, spiders form a dragline, a double thread that trails behind them. With it, they can return home quickly and easily. If danger should approach, spiders use the dragline to escape, dropping out of sight.

Silk Source

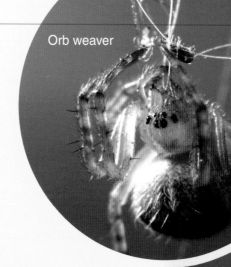

Orb weaver

Silk is still liquid as it leaves the spider's body. It emerges through spinnerets, which are flexible, fingerlike tubes, near the end of the body. As the spinnerets pull and bend the silk, the material hardens.

Silky World

Silk is the material of webs, traps, egg sacs, and burrow linings. It is produced by glands, as many as seven, deep inside a spider's body. Silk can be dry or sticky, fuzzy or smooth, thick or thin. Silk may look fragile, but it's amazingly sturdy. For added strength, spiders combine some threads to make thicker strands and may cover threads with a sticky substance.

Building Bridges

A silk bridge makes traveling between bushes and trees a lot easier. Standing in one place, spiders let out a thread for the wind to carry until it snags on another spot.

Orb weaver

Wonder Webs

Think of spider webs, and you may imagine a beautiful wheel with delicate spokes. This is the orb web, just one of the many kinds of webs that spiders build. The length of silk that goes into such a construction can be over 60 feet. Orb webs are the deadliest trap of all for flying insects.

Orb spider

Web City

Many spiders are loners. But social types live in colonies, numbering in the thousands. They create an enormous web that covers a tree, or they link webs to blanket a field.

Snap Trap

Certain spiders can build elastic rectangular webs that fold up. The spider waits, holding the collapsed web like a net in its front legs while hanging close to the ground by its back legs. When insects pass by, the spider drops the net over its victims.

Net casting spider

Funnel Tunnel

Funnel weavers trap insects through surprise. They build tornado-shaped webs that are flat and lacy on the top with a funnel in the center.

Nabbing Prey

All spiders have ways of capturing prey, but each species has its own method. Some spiders rely on their webs to grab prey; others are more aggressive. The latter spiders, the more active ones, are equipped with special tools: instead of a sticky net, they use their large, powerful jaws to capture meals. Raft spiders snatch their prey directly from the water, wiggling a leg to look like a worm.

Super Stalkers

A jumping spider is the most successful active hunter of all the arachnae. It stalks prey the way a cat stalks mice.

Spider Eat Spider

Some spiders eat other spiders. Lynx spiders do not build webs and do not have as good eyesight as jumping spiders. They wait for prey to go by and pounce, using venom to subdue their victims.

Tricky Trapdoor

A trapdoor spider digs a burrow and lines it with silk, then builds a door on top. This sneaky spider stays inside waiting. When potential prey is nearby, the trapdoor spider releases the trapdoor and attacks unsuspecting prey.

Tarantula Dance

Big, hairy spiders are called tarantulas. The name comes from the medieval Italian city of Taranto. The people there claimed that the bite of a spider made them dance wildly. The dance was called the tarantella, and the spider was named the tarantula. The South American bird-eating spider is the largest spider in the world. This type of tarantula has a 3-inch long body and 10-inch long legs.

True Tarantula

The true tarantula is the European wolf spider. They are nocturnal and usually hunt by waiting at the entrance of their burrows for prey to walk by.

Up a Tree

Tarantulas are good at climbing, because, like other wandering spiders, they have pads of hair on their feet. While they are up in trees, they capture frogs, birds, lizards, and even small snakes.

LOVED TO DEATH

Furry tarantulas, especially the Mexican red-kneed spider, have become so popular as pets that too many have been taken from the wild. Now, sales are being regulated, and some are bred in captivity.

Fight Club

Spiders don't get too friendly with one another. If two meet up, they're bound to fight, and it's a battle to the end.

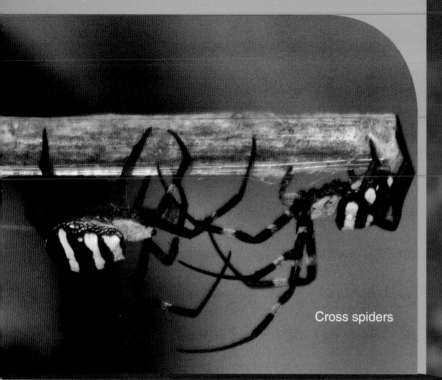

African baboon spider

Cross spiders

HAIRY SCARY

Some tarantulas have a hairy defense weapon. When threatened, the Chilean red-leg tarantula raises its lower body, vibrates its back legs, and scrapes off a mist of stinging, barbed hairs.

Staying Alive

Spiders have predators, such as frogs, toads, lizards, birds, and wasps. Disappearing is often the best defense. Hiding is another. One way that spiders hide is by making themselves look like other things. This is called mimicry. But if a spider can't escape, a battle begins. It raises its front legs and shows its fangs, hoping this will be enough to frighten the attacker.

Ant Act

Some spiders look and act like ants. These arachnids move their front legs as "antennae" and run in an antlike, zigzag fashion. Their disguise is so good, some live with real ants.

Ant spider

Ant

Tricky Spiders

Camouflage, or blending into the background, fools both predators and prey. Green lynx spiders know this trick. They always use green hunting grounds, so they just sit still on green leaves and wait for dinner.

Undercover

There are spiders that have markings like lichen, mold, and mosses that grow on trees. Pressed up against a tree, these spiders blend in with the bark and cast no shadow.

Fishing spider

Flower Power

Crab spiders use the power of flowers to snare prey. Also called flower spiders, these arachnids sit on flowers that match their body color, waiting for bees or butterflies to fly by.

Goldenrod crab spider

Behind the Blade

For the long-jawed orb weaver, posture is a life saver. Clinging to a blade of grass with one pair of legs, it simply becomes part of the grass until the danger has passed.

Spiderlings

There are billions upon billions of spiders on Earth, and more being born every minute. All female spiders lay eggs called spiderlings. Small spiders lay smaller and fewer eggs. Giant bird-eating spiders may lay up to 3,000 eggs, each the size of a pea.

Marbled orb spider

Sign Language

Male and female spiders communicate using unique signals. A male web spider may vibrate the silk strands of a female's web in a kind of code. Wandering spiders do a courtship dance.

Mother's Work

Female spiders are in charge of laying and fertilizing eggs: placing their eggs on a disc of silk and then fertilizing them with the male spiders' fluid. Next, the female spins silk around the eggs to make a protective sac.

Wolf spider

Sac Hatch

Spiderlings break out of their eggs and remain in their egg sac until they are fully developed. If food is scarce, they may eat a brother or sister before going on their way.

Protective Mamas

Some spiders protect their egg sacs. The nursery-web spider builds a silk tent for her babies and guards them until they all scatter.

Vicious Venom

The black widow's venom is one of the deadliest. It's about 15 times more potent than rattlesnake venom. Humans only experience discomfort for a couple of days.

Danger Down Under

Australia is home to one of the most venomous spiders in the world: the Sydney funnel-web spider. Its bite first causes unbearable pain, then convulsions and a coma.

Bad Bites

Spiders bite—that's why they have fangs. They also kill their prey with poison. A bite to humans, however, is almost always harmless, unless it is from one of these more venomous spiders. Fortunately, deaths from spiders are extremely rare.

Sydney funnel-web spider

Wretched Recluse

The brown recluse has a nasty poisonous bite that grows. Starting out as a small black spot, the area of dead, peeling skin can expand to six inches.

Special Selection

What you picture in your mind when you hear the word "spider" may not be what you actually see. Because there are so many species of spiders, you can be sure that they look very different from one another. Then, too, they don't all act the same. Here, you get a peek at an assortment of artful arthropods.

Sand Surfer

The wheel spider of the Southern African desert digs a burrow in the sand. When first starting to dig, it can be preyed on by a parasitic wasp. To escape, it tucks itself into a ball and rolls away.

Spiny orb weaver

Water World

Sea spiders aren't really spiders but they are related and have similar behaviors to wandering spiders. There are about 600 species of sea spiders.

Disappearing Act

Daddy-longlegs spiders look as frail as feathers, but they get around—especially in cellars and dark corners, where they hang upside-down in loose webs.

Long Leap

Only a fifth of an inch long, jumping spiders can jump forty times their body length. Jumping off strong back legs, they can even leap to catch flying insects in midair!

Living with Spiders

Spiders can look pretty scary, with all those legs and eyes. Some people are really afraid of them, a fear called arachnophobia. But spiders aren't that big of a danger to people. They are actually helpful to us. People who study spiders are called arachnologists.

Bug Buster

Spiders eat so many insects that they could make good farmhands. If spiders can be introduced into fields to protect crops, they may be able to help decrease the use of pesticides.

Garden spider

ARACHNOPHOBIA

Arachnophobia is one of the most common fears. With the help of a therapist, sufferers can overcome their fear through treatment called systematic desensitization. Eventually these people conquer their phobia when they are capable of holding a live spider.

Bite Fright

Getting bitten by a spider can be scary. If you are healthy, most likely you will be all right though it is recommended that you visit the doctor.

Tarantula

Black widow spider

29

GLOSSARY

Abdomen: In spiders, the last body part; behind the cephalothorax.

Arachnids: Any member of the scientific classification Arachnida, including spiders, scorpions, mites, and ticks.

Arachnologist: A person who studies spiders.

Arachnophobia: Fear of spiders.

Arthropods: Animals, such as insects and spiders, that have an exoskeleton (a skeleton outside their body). Arthropods usually have segmented bodies and jointed legs.

Camouflage: The way an animal disguises and protects itself by blending with its surroundings.

Carapace: A hard exterior skeleton, or exoskeleton, that protects a spider's soft body parts.

Carnivore: An animal that eats the flesh of other animals.

Cephalothorax: In spiders, a combined head and thorax; the first of two body parts.

Dragline: A double thread of silk that trails behind spiders to help them return home quickly if danger approaches.

Egg sac: A protective sac made of silk that some mother spiders spin around their eggs to protect them.

Exoskeleton: A hard exterior skeleton, called a carapace, which protects a spider's soft body parts. An exoskeleton does not grow; it must be molted and a new one formed.

Fangs: The long appendages, or arms, above a spider's mouth that hold a gland at their tip that produces poison.

Insect: A class of anthropods with three body parts: head, thorax, and abdomen. These creatures also have six legs and typically have wings.

Mimicry: The resemblance of a living creature to some other thing, such as a branch, flower, or other animal, so as to deceive prey or predators.

Molt: To cast off periodically hair, feathers, shell, horns, or an outer layer. A spider molts its carapace when it outgrows it.

Mygalomorphs: Large spiders, such as tarantulas, that move their jaws up and down rather than from side to side.

Pedipalps: Leglike appendages on each side of a spider's mouth, used to hold prey.

Pirate spiders: Spiders that eat other spiders.

Poison: A venom that kills or injures. Some spiders have a venomous bite.

Predator: An animal that hunts other animals for food.

Prey: An animal that is hunted by other animals.

Regeneration: Regrowth, as when a spider grows a new leg or carapace to replace a lost or damaged one.

Silk: An elastic thread produced by spiders and used to construct webs, egg sacs, and draglines.

Spiderlings: Baby spiders.

Spinnerets: Flexible, fingerlike tubes near the end of a spider's body that produce silk.

True spiders: Spiders whose jaws move from side to side; common spiders.

Venom: A poisonous that kills or injures. Some spiders have a venomous bite.

Vibrations: Quivering or trembling motions that can be heard or felt.

Wandering spiders: Spiders that actively hunt for prey and do not spin webs.

Web: A network of fine strands of silk formed to snare prey. Spiders produce many kinds of webs, including funnel webs, elastic rectangular webs, and orb webs.

Web-building spiders: Spiders that spin sticky webs and wait for prey to become entangled there.